HANDLING THE DIFFICULT EMPLOYEE

Solving Performance Problems

Marty Brounstein

A FIFTY-MINUTE™ SERIES BOOK

Viva Books Private Limited
New Delhi • Mumbai • Chennai • Kolkata • Bangalore • Hyderabad

First Indian Edition 2004

VIVA BOOKS PRIVATE LIMITED

- 4262/3 Ansari Road, Daryaganj, New Delhi 110 002
  E-mail: viva@vivagroupindia.net
- 215-216 New Apollo Estate, 2nd Floor, Mogra Lane, Andheri (E), Mumbai 400 069
  E-mail: vivamumbai@vivagroupindia.net
- Jamal Fazal Chambers, 26 Greams Road, Chennai 600 006
  E-mail: vivachennai@vivagroupindia.net
- B-103, Jindal Towers, 21/1A/3 Darga Road, Kolkata 700 017
  E-mail: vivakolkata@vivagroupindia.net
- 7 GF, Sovereign Park Apts., 56-58 K.R. Road, Basavanagudi, Bangalore 560 004
  E-mail: vivabangalore@vivagroupindia.net

Published by arrangement with

Crisp Publications, Inc.
1200 Hamilton Court,
Menlo Park
CA 94025
USA

Credits:
Editor: Bev Manber
Layout and Composition: ExecuStaff
Cover Design: Amy Shayne and Fifth Street Design
Artwork: Ralph Mapson

ISBN 81-7649-574-3

Published by Vinod Vasishtha for Viva Books Private Limited, 4262/3 Ansari Road, Daryaganj, New Delhi 110 002 and printed & bound by Raj Press, R-3 Inderpuri, New Delhi 110 012.

LEARNING OBJECTIVES FOR:

HANDLING THE DIFFICULT EMPLOYEE

The objectives for *Handling the Difficult Employee* are listed below. They have been developed to guide you, the reader, to the core issues covered in this book.

Objectives

- ❑ **1) To clarify how to intervene**
- ❑ **2) To explain the intervention conference**
- ❑ **3) To advise regarding termination**

Assessing Your Progress

In addition to the learning objectives, Crisp Learning has developed an **assessment** that covers the fundamental information presented in this book. A 25-item, multiple choice and true-false questionnaire allows the reader to evaluate his or her comprehension of the subject matter. To learn how to obtain a copy of this assessment, please call **1-800-442-7477** and ask to speak with a Customer Service Representative.

Assessments should not be used in any employee selection process.

PREFACE

Many supervisors and managers face the task of dealing with difficult employees: those who often come in late, don't work hard, procrastinate, or keep morale low. This book shows how to determine the causes of employee performance problems and suggests what intervention steps to take. Rather than dictate performance changes, managers are encouraged to give constructive feedback to help employees improve work ethic and morale.

A six-step Intervention Model offers good suggestions about communication, a plan of improvement, and problem resolution. The Intervention Model also shows how to deal effectively with discipline and termination situations. All employee performance issues, including management responsibility, are discussed in detailed case studies.

Marty Brounstein

ABOUT THE AUTHOR

Marty Brounstein is a consultant and trainer who specializes in management development, career development, customer service, sexual harassment and diversity. This book is the subject of one of his most well-received seminars.

Brounstein is a former human resources executive. He holds an M.S. degree in Industrial Relations and has over a dozen years of experience in management and education. This is his second book to be published by Crisp Publications; he previously co-authored *Effective Recruiting Strategies.*

Dedication—

To my Frances,

For all your love and support.
I couldn't have done this without you.

CONTENTS

PART I

Defining Difficult Employees

MANAGEMENT'S RESPONSIBILITY

For as long as there have been managers, there have been difficult employees. As a supervisor or manager, if you have not yet experienced a difficult employee, wait—sooner or later you will.

Before we explore *what is* a difficult employee, let's address a couple of management issues. Please fill in the blanks in the statements below:

1. A ________________ is someone who has to work through and with others to get the job done and achieve results. Someone in this position is responsible not only for his or her own work, but also for work produced by the group and its individual members.

2. A key part of a manager's job is to manage the ________________ of his or her staff; for that produces the results for which a manager is held accountable.

A vast number of titles, from supervisor to president, exist for the function of manager. *Manager,* as used in this book refers to someone who has people-reporting responsibilities and is, therefore, responsible for more than his or her own work. The manager's most important responsibility is to manage the performance of his or her employees; through the employees the results will happen.

Therefore, the first step, before handling any problem employee situation, is to recognize that managing the performance of others is a key part of what management at any level is about. As a manager, your job entails more than your own work. If any of the people you supervise is not doing his or her job well, you share in the responsibility of that below-par performance. Until you recognize this fact, you cannot begin to resolve employee performance problems.

The answers:

1. manager
2. performance

DEFINITION OF THE DIFFICULT EMPLOYEE

A difficult employee is someone who does not fully meet the performance standards of his or her job, as needed by the organization, and especially by the manager. A difficult employee is not necessarily a bad person, but someone whose level of performance is not up to the standards. The problem may be with one area of the employee's job or with many areas. If the standards of the job are not met, a performance problem exists.

In fact, you may have been a problem employee at one time or another. Many, if not most, employees—including managers—have times when they are not doing something as well as their bosses need or expect. Remember, when this below-standard situation occurs, a potential problem employee is upon us—not necessarily a bad person.

Your goal as a manager is to take the *problem* out of the employee, not to take out the employee. Termination is the quickest way to solve an immediate performance problem. However, if it is used as the main strategy every time an employee makes a mistake or does not do something well, it will be very difficult for you to find employees to work for you.

Turnover, especially when done in this abrupt manner, is extremely costly. Here are some of the major costs to an organization from this kind of turnover.

- Time and money to recruit and hire a new employee
- Re-training to bring the new employee up-to-speed
- Salary and benefit costs already paid out to the terminated employee
- Unemployment compensation and, potentially, severance pay
- Damage to morale of the remaining employees
- Possible wrongful termination lawsuit

On the other hand, if a manager tries to improve a performance problem situation, more often than not improved performance occurs. By far, it is the cheapest way to handle a problem employee, and the best way to prevent the tragedy of excessive turnover.

DEGREES OF DIFFICULT EMPLOYEES

Difficult employees come in varying degrees, from relatively simple to very difficult. Following is a description of the most common types or degrees of difficult employees:

The New Employee

The new employee is a problem employee: She or he starts out not knowing what is expected and takes a while to come up to a competent performance level. This person needs training and guidance to function at the level we need the job performed.

With your guidance and support, you can minimize mistakes by, and your concerns about, the new employee. Without management effort, this small degree of problem employee may get bigger, not better, over time.

The Inconsistent Employee

The inconsistent employee generally performs in streaks: good days, then bad days; good weeks, then bad weeks; even good months, then not so good months. This individual is usually a capable performer who can do most aspects of the job well, but who does not do them on a consistent basis.

The inconsistent employee thrives best under a manager who takes a laissez-faire approach, or who relies on short-term memory to monitor performance. As a result, this employee performs best just before his or her annual evaluation. Then, after a good review and a decent raise, his or her performance slips down again.

DEGREES OF DIFFICULT EMPLOYEES (continued)

The Unbalanced Employee

The unbalanced employee is generally very strong in one aspect of the job—most often technical skill or ingenuity—and quite weak in another aspect of the job—most often behavior. This employee is often a very talented worker, but due to difficulty with conduct or work relationships, lacks balance in performance.

The unbalanced employee usually appears in one of three versions: antagonist, maverick or cynic.

Antagonist types are usually at odds with someone else or with many someones. When at odds, their tone and manner sometimes publicly as well as privately, are harsh or attacking—put downs, insults, criticism. They rarely have trouble speaking their mind, and when they do, other people often feel emotionally wounded.

Maverick types are usually off working in their own direction, not caring or trying to adhere to the group's rules. A good example of this type of unbalanced employee was the character Hawkeye Pierce, played by Alan Alda, in the popular television show *MASH.* Pierce was a brilliant surgeon who didn't care about following army regulations or orders, or working peacefully with people he did not like. This maverick was at times quite a disruptive influence for his commanding officer.

Cynics are often the *rotten apples* who can spoil the others in the barrel. They are often critical of management decisions or of efforts to help the group. Their remarks are touched with cynicism and are frequently passed quietly around the work unit. Then, almost automatically, any idea or decision that the cynic thinks is bad, is perceived by the group as bad.

The Mediocre Employee

The mediocre employee performs the basics of the job; she or he handles routine tasks at the minimum level expected. The employee does no high quality work and makes no effort to do more. In times of great need or special projects, this mediocre employee is usually low on the list of people to whom a manager will turn for help.

The Marginal Employee

The marginal employee falls below minimum expectations in most of the critical aspects of the job. This degree of problem employee tends to slide by, mostly wasting time, not working productively. More often than not, other than when conduct is the problem, this employee is somewhat quiet and not very visible. The marginal employee thrives best in a large department where it is easy to get lost in the crowd.

The Intolerable Employee

The intolerable employee does very little work right, or does little work on time; his or her output is so very low, or absenteeism very high, or his or her behavior is disruptive to others. This is the employee whose manager can no longer tolerate the situation. At this stage, the manager often storms into the Human Resources Department and demands that immediate, formal disciplinary action be carried out, if not immediate dismissal. This manager usually tolerated the poor performance for so long and generally allowed this problem employee to grow into an intolerable and severe problem.

As a manager, the longer you wait to address a performance problem, the harder it will be to deal with it constructively and the worse the problem becomes. Employees do not start out as marginal or intolerable performers. Most often, they grow into these severe degrees of problems when little corrective effort was made while their performance was inconsistent, unbalanced or becoming mediocre.

In the 1980s, wrongful termination lawsuits became a fairly common practice, with employers losing many more cases than they won. The 1990s have reaffirmed the highly competitive economic climate we live in. In today's business world—in the public sector as well as in the private sector—managers, more than ever, need to effectively manage the performance of their people.

Recognizing this important management responsibility, and understanding what constitutes a problem or difficult employee, are important requisites for successfully resolving performance problems and achieving positive results.

REMEMBER THE MESSAGE

Fill in the blank. If you, as a manager, work with an employee to improve a performance problem, the most likely outcome is that performance will

__________________.

Of course, the answer is *improve.* Besides the employee, the person who has the greatest influence on an employee's performance is the manager. If you, as manager, think the employee is hopeless, then most likely worse, not better, performance will occur. When performance problems occur, your efforts to deal with them will often be a self-fulfilling prophecy.

Improvement is the most desirable result of your efforts. That is why reminding ourselves of the following message is important.

MOST PEOPLE WANT TO AND TRY TO DO A GOOD JOB

A Quick Assessment for Managers

Please answer the following questions:

1. Do you want to, and try to, do a good job? ____________________

2. If the employees in your work area were asked if they want to, and try to, do a good job, what would most of them answer? ____________

____

I have asked these questions of hundreds of managers and the overwhelming response has been *yes*. The vast majority of people want to, and try to, do a good job.

3. If you are not doing something well on your job, would you want to know about it? Do you think this would be true of most employees? ________

____

____

When asked these questions, managers have answered unanimously *yes*. Why? The most common response has been, "So I can have a chance to make whatever corrections or improvements are needed."

These responses reflect why the **MESSAGE** is so important to remember, when you are dealing with a problem employee situation. Problem employees are *people*. Despite the problems you are having with such individuals, most problem employees desire and intend to do a good job, and would like the chance to improve when they are not performing well.

As a manager, remember this important **MESSAGE**, which will help you approach a problem employee situation in a positive and constructive manner. Focus on making improvements—a self-fulfilling prophecy worth having.

COMMON WARNING SIGNS

Here are fourteen signs managers have stated that employees commonly exhibit, indicating a performance problem is developing:

1. **Output decrease.** The amount of work getting done decreases. Sales or production are below normal.

2. **Work quality.** Errors increase. Work is sloppy and sometimes incomplete.

3. **Due dates missed.** Assignments and/or projects are late, or not completed.

4. **Little or no initiative is shown.** The employee does not start to work without being pushed or reminded.

5. **Tougher tasks and assignments are avoided.** The employee puts off or complains about the more difficult jobs. Often, the employee's effort goes into getting someone else to do the work.

6. **Complaints increase.** The employee considers decisions that are made, tasks that are worked on, others' efforts, etc., to be wrong much of the time.

7. **Interaction with others decreases.** The employee turns quiet at meetings or more often works alone.

8. **Following and/or taking directions becomes difficult.** Instructions have to be repeated often. The employee frequently voices reasons why something cannot be done.

9. **Defensiveness or irritability increases.** Having calm and rational conversations with this employee becomes more difficult. Mood swings become more pronounced.

10. **Cooperation diminishes.** Getting along and working with other employees becomes more difficult. Conflicts start to happen.

11. **Others are blamed for mistakes or failures.** The employee does not accept responsibility for his or her actions and is quick to find fault with others.

12. **Absences from his/her desk increase.** The person is not around when needed, and often no one knows where to find the individual.

13. **Negative feedback from others increases.** Other employees or customers tell you about difficulties and disappointments they have in trying to deal with your employee.

14. **Absenteeism and/or tardiness increases.**

Most managers recognize these problem signs developing. Most likely, you have too. The key in resolving performance problems, in taking the *problem* out of the employee, is to recognize these in their early stages—catch them early when they are easiest to correct.

Unfortunately, many managers choose to take a Management-By-Wishing-and-Avoidance approach when these signs occur: The manager wishes the problem employee would just straighten up and avoids dealing directly with the issue. "It's really not so bad" is heard often from such managers. The truth is, employees do not read minds; when performance problems are ignored, they tend to get worse, not better.

Other managers practice a Management-By-Threat or Write-'Em-Up approach when they see these signs. With this approach, yelling, screaming, ultimatums and disciplinary letters to the personnel file are tactics commonly used to address the problem. The employee, stunned or surprised by the actions, becomes defensive or confrontational. This punitive approach tends to provoke covert resistance and mistrust, and leaves the problem still intact.

As mentioned before, most employees want to know when they are not doing something well. If you let them know while the problem is small in scope, and work with them to correct the situation (Management-By-Corrective-Intervention), you have a good chance of seeing performance improve.

SIX-STEP INTERVENTION MODEL

This book will give you a six-step intervention model to deal successfully with problem employee situations:

Intervention Model

STEP 1 Identify and define the performance problem.

STEP 2 Explain the impact of the problem.

STEP 3 Analyze the reasons for the problem.

STEP 4 Define the expected performance standard.

STEP 5 Explore ideas for a solution.

STEP 6 Write an improvement plan, with action plans and target dates.

THREE KEY PRINCIPLES

This intervention model works if three key principles are followed:

1. Take Corrective, NOT Punitive, Actions

The emphasis here is on improvement. When performance is not up to standard, efforts are directed at exploring what is wrong and, most importantly, what needs to be done to turn the performance around.

Corrective efforts focus on actions the employee, with the manager's support, can do, not on what they should not do. Punishment may work well with children or criminals but it often creates fear, resentment and resistance in employees. Punishment does not tell the employee how to improve his or her performance.

2. Counsel and Coach Before Using Discipline

The point is that the manager makes an effort, often done a few times, to bring performance concerns to the attention of the employee in a timely manner. The manager coaches and counsels the employee, to work out ways for improvement *before* any form of disciplinary action is considered—severe circumstances being the exception. Disciplinary action is reserved for situations when improvement in a reasonable amount of time does not occur.

Discipline should come as a corrective and logical consequence, in line with intervention efforts—a consequence spelled out in advance. No surprises, no "lowering the boom," or any other arbitrary actions have occurred. Even under these circumstances, action plans to improve performance are developed.

3. Be Firm, Be Fair and Do Care

Address problems directly and timely, while they are in their early stages. (*Firm*)

Carry out appropriate consequences, as necessary. For example, "Until this work is done accurately, you will not take on that special project you've been requesting." Provide positive, not just negative, consequences. (*Fair*)

Most importantly, show concern for the individual. There is a person connected to the problem employee. (*Care*)

This third key principle is about being assertive. Sometimes employees need to be told when they are not doing well. *Firm, fair* and *care* are the watchwords to follow.

* * *

In applying these principles to the intervention model, termination comes only after all other good faith efforts to improve performance have been exhausted. Termination must be for *just cause*: The reason for dismissal must be clear to all involved, especially to the employee.

Termination can often be prevented. Employees usually improve their performance or, alternatively, decide to go elsewhere when they do not think improvement can happen. Bitterness and tension are minimized; sometimes manager and employee feel a sense of relief, even if termination is necessary. One way or another, a performance problem situation has been positively resolved.

Remember:

Improving performance is what it is all about!

PART II

The Intervention Model

STEP 1: IDENTIFY AND DEFINE THE PERFORMANCE PROBLEM

The warning signs are there if an employee not performing up to standard is upon you. To talk to the employee about this problem will require specifics. What is the issue involved? What are the examples that describe what has been happening with the person's performance?

Intervening to address a performance problem situation begins when you answer these questions that identify and define the problem to the employee. This is the first step of the Intervention Model. It is critical—if the employee does not clearly understand the problem, your efforts to use the rest of the model will be unsuccessful.

ISSUES OF PERFORMANCE

Focus on the performance in question. Performance issues can be categorized into three areas: attendance, work and job-related behaviors.

Attendance

Issues most important to attendance are:

- Punctuality
- Being at work

If an employee is tardy or absent, and it has a negative effort on his or her ability to get a job done, an attendance problem exists.

With short term absenteeism—a few days or less of absence at a time—focus your attention on the pattern and frequency of absence, to determine if a potential problem exists. *Pattern* refers to being absent around weekends or at critical times, such as deadline dates for important projects. *Frequency* is the number of days the employee is absent within a set time period.

In both cases, the key is to explain the impact of the employee's absence. When there is a pattern of absence, the employee's credibility and reliability are impacted and important assignments may be delayed. When frequency is too high, completing work when it is needed, and requiring others to do extra work to cover for the absent person pose some of the greatest impact.

With a potential absentee problem, it is critical that you avoid discussing why the person has not been present. Abuse of leave, e.g., when an employee calls in sick when she or he is not ill, is very hard to prove. Trying to prove it puts you, as a manager, in the position of detective, judge and jury—a no-win position.

Asking employees to bring in a doctor's note for a day or two of absence keeps you on an "I don't trust you" path—a path that leads to conflict, rather than resolution. And, the resulting charges for unnecessary office visits help drive up your company's medical insurance costs. If the employee has a short-term illness, aspirin and rest are usually the best prescriptions to follow treatment which does not require a medical degree to figure out.

Although knowing why an employee is absent can be helpful for understanding the problem, being at work is most significant for having good performance. This is where your attention should be. If absences are interfering with an employee's job getting done, an attendance problem needs to be addressed.

Work Employees Do

With the work or tasks of employees, the main issues to manage are:

- Output
- Quality
- Accuracy
- Timeliness

Most of what is important in the work employees do relates to one or more of these areas. If not enough work is getting done, or it is not getting done well enough, or it is not done correctly, or it does not get done when required, then a performance problem exists, which needs to be addressed.

Job-Related Behaviors

The last category of performance issues deals with conduct and interpersonal relations. It is often the area managers are most uncomfortable addressing. Their apprehension is often caused by difficulty in distinguishing behaviors from personality traits; they fear they will wind up in a personality conflict. Despite their apprehension, managers need to address an employee's behavior problems; this third performance issue category often has the most negative impact on a group's overall performance.

With job-related behavior issues, the key is to describe what the employee is doing—observable, specific actions. Avoid labels and vague generalizations.

Some of the common labels put on perceived problem employees are *lazy, stupid, unmotivated, immature* and *bad attitude.* These labels do not tell specifically what the employee is doing. Vague, inflammatory comments, with no substance to back them up, do not help someone understand his or her performance problem. Furthermore, such labels give the message that the employee is flawed beyond hope and that the manager has no responsibility to try to improve the performance of this hopeless individual.

Without examples describing how the person behaved, even more substantive comments such as, "Your lack of cooperation is hurting the team," or "Your demeanor in front of customers is not very professional," sound like vague criticism, rather than constructive feedback. Again, the key with behavior problems is to describe the employee's actions in *tangible* and *specific* terms.

Exercise #1: Describe Appropriate Behavior

Use the statements below to write appropriate behavior descriptions. Describe what the person might be doing, as it relates to the statement. Be creative. Refer to samples on page 65 for comparison.

1. Mary often does not cooperate with her department team.

____

____

____

____

____

2. Steve's demeanor in front of customers is not very friendly.

____

____

____

____

____

CASE STUDY #1

Practice by analyzing the following case:

> ## *Jim*
>
> Jim's manager, Bob, was talking about problems he was having with Jim. Unfortunately, Bob's description about Jim's performance was in the form of negative labels and vague generalizations. See if you can identify them in the paragraph below.
>
> **According to Bob:**
>
> "Jim can be a very disagreeable person at times. He's also disorganized in his work. In addition, while I think he is bright enough to do the job, he lacks drive and motivation. Overall, I just don't think he is a very reliable employee."

Labels About Jim

List four labels and generalizations about Jim's behavior.

1. ______________________________

2. ______________________________

3. ______________________________

4. ______________________________

Compare your answers with those on page 65.

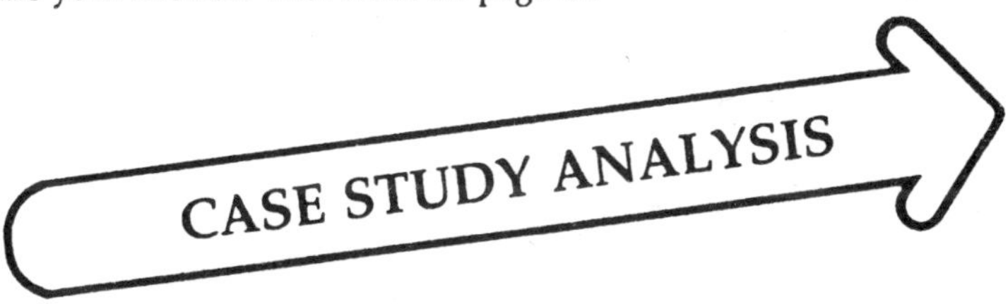

CASE STUDY ANALYSIS

After Bob learned how to identify and define problems more accurately, he revised his description. In his improved version that follows, identify three of Jim's job-related behavior problems. Then check your answers against those on page 65.

"During the last two months, when giving Jim directions on assignments, he often responds by telling me what can't be done. When new ideas are introduced, he is quick to point out why they won't work, without listening to them all the way through or giving them a fair try."

"Sometimes Jim is required to make customer deliveries. He often takes twice as long as would normally be expected to do them. For example, last Friday he went into an area he was unfamiliar with; he did not take the map we provide with him. Two hours later, he called asking for directions. Then last Tuesday, even in an area he knew, he arranged the deliveries so that he went from one end of the city and back again, instead of doing them in order of close proximity."

"In the office, Jim often sits at his desk and does not do anything until he is told to get to work. During the last month, his lunch breaks have become longer than the allowable one hour. He usually returns an average of 15 minutes late."

1. ____________________

____

2. ____________________

____

3. ____________________

____

WHAT ARE NOT ISSUES OF PERFORMANCE

When you describe what the person did as it relates to doing his or her job, in observable behaviors, you are focused on issues of performance. When you talk about what you think the employee is like, you are describing issues of personality—not issues of performance. Whether you like or dislike the individual is irrelevant when you manage performance. Regardless of what you may think about an employee's traits, motives or intentions, focusing on these characteristics leads you down the road of personality conflicts and not on the path to performance improvement.

Personal background is also not an issue of performance. Gender, age, racial, ethnic and religious background, and any other factors related to an employee's personal background, have nothing to do with his or her performance. If you think one of these factors is the cause of the problem, you are no longer focused on what the employee is, or is not, doing as it relates to the job. Instead, your focus is on who that person is or looks to be—actions that will cause discrimination.

GIVE CONSTRUCTIVE FEEDBACK

To identify and define the problem to the employee, you will be required to give constructive feedback. We will start with a few definitions:

Feedback: Information or input returned to the other person

Criticism: Passing of unfavorable judgment, directed at a person

Praise: Passing of favorable judgment, directed at a person

Positive and negative feedback are both forms of constructive feedback. Different from praise or criticism, constructive feedback is based on evidence, not on judgments or opinions. It is directed at a person's performance, not on the person.

Here are guidelines for giving constructive feedback:

1. *Be specific;* relate the feedback to an issue of performance (i.e., attendance, tasks, behavior or some other action). Start your feedback by identifying the issue: State it in one sentence. It is often helpful to begin the statement with an "I" message, such as "I have noticed" or "I have observed." This helps to focus your feedback right on the issue of performance. Compare these two examples:

   a) You have been doing a lot less work lately.
   b) Lately, I have noticed a decrease in your output.

   In statement a) the focus is on you, whereas in statement b) the focus is on the person's output—the performance issue.

2. *Give examples* or other supporting evidence.
   Examples and supporting evidence provide the definition and substance behind the issue identified in your opening statement. Keep your language from sounding biased, harsh or judgmental—just report the facts.

3. *Express appreciation* when giving feedback on POSITIVE situations.
   Identifying what an employee has done well is reinforcing for that person. Including a statement of appreciation provides a reward for his or her effort. People like to be appreciated for the efforts they make.

4. *Express concern* when giving feedback on NEGATIVE situations. Expressing concern about substandard performance lets employees know you care about them as individuals. If employees know you care, they are more likely to care and to work to improve their performance problem.

5. *Be direct and sincere.* Get to the point, and do not beat around the proverbial bush—mean what you say and say what you mean. Your tone of voice is critical for sounding sincere.

   Along with being genuine, avoid giving mixed messages—avoid "yes but" statements such as, "You have been doing a good job, but I am concerned about your work on . . ." These kinds of messages negate anything said before, and the sincerity of the message-giver comes into question.

   When the essence of your message deals with a negative performance situation, avoid being compelled to say something positive. Save the positive feedback for times when the employee makes positive efforts.

6. *Give feedback directly,* NOT through messengers. In both positive and negative situations, feedback given to third parties to pass on to the intended person dilutes the value and sincerity of the message.

   Feedback works best when it is given face-to-face and privately. Do not use electronic mail, voice mail and memos to give constructive feedback. On occasion, with positive feedback, a public forum can work well as a form of recognition; exercise caution so you do not embarrass the employee.

7. *Give timely feedback, without delay.* Timely feedback means giving it as soon as possible and, most importantly, as soon as you are ready. Sometimes that may be the next day instead of the next minute. Attempting to give constructive feedback when you are emotionally charged up or when you do not have all your facts in order, will most likely turn your effort from constructive to destructive.

   However, if you put off giving the feedback until weeks later—or at the annual review period—it will have far less impact on the employee. Important news that arrives late becomes less important as time passes.

GIVE CONSTRUCTIVE FEEDBACK (continued)

8. *Distribute feedback equally in effort*—when things go wrong AND when things go right. This last guideline is about working as hard to catch people doing something right as you are working to catch them doing something wrong. For most employees, this means distributing positive feedback more often than negative feedback.

   When this kind of equal effort is made, the times when negative feedback needs to be given is taken far more constructively. Employees know if they work to improve, their efforts are noticed and recognized by you, and thus they are more likely to try.

The Significant Events List on the following page is a tool helpful in tracking employee performance efforts, and in tracking your efforts to give constructive feedback. The idea is to make a small notation when something occurs—if you write more than two sentences, you are writing too much. The list serves as a tracking mechanism as well as a memory jogger. Follow this one simple rule:

Record nothing that you have not already communicated directly to the employee.

Significant Events List

List and briefly describe the major accomplishments, actions and behaviors related to job performance—from the positive to the negative—as they occur during the course of the performance evaluation period.

EMPLOYEE: ______________________________

DATE	EVENT

Exercise #2: Feedback Identification

Identify whether the following statements are examples of *praise, criticism* or *constructive feedback.* See page 66 to check your answers.

1. I am really disappointed with your efforts lately. You know what I mean.

____

2. I want you to understand how that effort with the customer did not go well. First off, the customer's concerns were not really acknowledged. While you tried to get him to tell you his problem, you did not express empathy with how he was feeling. Secondly, he did not agree with the solution you proposed, and you did not explore the reasons why not.

____

3. You did a real nice job on that last project. Way to go. ________________

4. Your recent extra efforts in helping the team have really paid off. Your efforts helped us maintain our output levels, when nearly half the staff was out with the flu. In addition, the time you took to train the new employee has helped him come up-to-speed quickly. Thanks so much for giving that extra effort. ________________

5. That presentation you gave was a waste of time. You were very boring.

____

Now practice by writing constructive feedback as it would apply to the scenarios presented below. Feel free to be creative and add any information you need to give it more substance.

1. George is one of your new employees. Within his first two weeks on the job, he learned five of the key duties of the job, took the initiative to help other staff members, and completed all assignments given to him accurately and on time. What will you say to George?

____

____

____

____

2. Melissa is good at greeting customers warmly. However, she is well below standard in keeping up with customer calls. In addition, the customer file information she is to keep up-to-date is more than two weeks behind. What will you say to Melissa?

____

____

____

____

3. After hearing your staff grumble about the extra work they have to do because Roberto is often absent, you checked the attendance records and found that Roberto has been absent ten days in the past three months. All have been single days of absence. What will you say to Roberto?

____

____

____

____

You can check your responses with those of the author on page 66.

STEP 2: EXPLAIN THE IMPACT OF THE PROBLEM

After you identify and define the problem, your next step is to define the impact of the problem; in other words, tell the employee the effect of his or her performance problem. The key to this is not to say there has been negative impact, but to describe specifically what the impact has been.

For example, instead of saying, "Your absenteeism is hurting productivity," say, "Because of the frequency of your absences, John, Bill and Sue have had to cover your desk to get the work done. This has resulted in all three putting in an average of five hours of overtime a week over the last month to also maintain their own workloads."

As you evaluate the problem, be prepared to define its impact on such factors as:

- Productivity and efficiency
- Quality
- Service
- Any other important business aspects

Performance problems also impact people greatly. Explain the effect on those most affected, such as:

You, the Manager

Your energy level and effectiveness are often negatively impacted when you have a problem employee situation. Since you are ultimately responsible for the work your employees do, if one of your staff's performance is down, so is yours. Also, your time with this employee is not being spent as productively as you want.

Be careful not to say that your time is being wasted on this problem situation. That would send the message that you do not care and do not have time for this employee. The key idea to communicate is how your time is being used with the employee. There are far more positive and productive endeavors that you would prefer and need to spend time working on together, rather than trying to resolve performance problems.

The Employee

Certainly a performance problem situation has impact on the employee involved. His or her credibility comes into question; advancement potential, as appropriate, is also in doubt. Help the problem employee understand that his or her value to the team is down when his or her level of performance is down.

The Department or Unit

One of the biggest areas of impact is with co-workers. Morale and productivity are often adversely affected when a performance problem exists within the group. Again, make sure you give specific examples as to how others in the unit are impacted.

Others

Performance problems often affect others outside the work group, such as employees in other departments, customers and the organization itself. The organization is most often impacted when the person's position is a prominent one within the organization. Tell employees of any feedback you receive. The more concrete your evidence, the more clearly the employee will understand the problem.

Once you define the impact of the performance problem, an employee will often acknowledge the situation. Problem employees are not always aware of the impact of their performance. Reporting the facts on impact frequently serves as a good eye-opener for them.

NOTE: If the impact of a performance problem is small, spend little time addressing the issue. For example, Shelly comes in late to work, on the average, four times a month. She puts in quite a few hours on a regular basis, and her inconsistent punctuality has little effect on her work or that of others.

Making an issue out of little problems tends to aggravate them and turn them into big ones. Match your time spent addressing an issue with its impact. Managers often ignore the big impact situations and use overkill on the little ones. Keep the molehills from becoming mountains.

Define the Impact

Define specifically the impact of a performance problem situation you know about. Include its impact on you, your department and co-workers. Did the problem impact productivity or morale? How?

STEP 3: ANALYZE THE REASONS FOR THE PROBLEM

The next step in the intervention effort is to figure out the reasons for the performance problem. This analysis, which the employee can often help you figure out, can be helpful in working out an improvement plan. Quite simply, the better you understand the causes of a problem, the easier it is for you to develop a workable solution.

10 Reasons Employees Do Not Perform up-to-Standard

1. They do not know how or what they should do.
2. The reward or consequence is for not doing what they should do.
3. They think they are doing just fine.
4. They think their way, not your way, is better, and it is not.
5. There is no negative consequence to them for poor performance.
6. They have obstacles limiting their performance.
7. They do not want to do the job, or know why they should do it.
8. They fear a negative consequence.
9. They are, in essence, punished for doing what they are supposed to do.
10. They think something else is more important.

Exercise #3: Performance Assessments

Following are three of the ten common reasons why employees do not perform up-to-standard. For each reason, give two reasons why this problem might exist. Then give a couple of ideas as to what you, as a manager, can do to improve each situation.

1. They do not know how or what they should do. Why?

   ____

   ____

   What can the manager do to help?

   ____

   ____

2. The reward or consequence is for not doing what they should do. Why?

   ____

   ____

   What can the manager do to help?

   ____

   ____

3. They think they are doing just fine. Why?

   ____

   ____

   What can the manager do to help?

   ____

   ____

Check your answers and ideas with those of the author on pages 67 to 71 in the Appendix. (If you want to practice assessing the remaining seven reasons on your own, the author has provided answers and ideas for these as well.)

EXAMINE YOUR INFLUENCE

As you have seen in the past few pages, you, as manager, have tremendous influence on employee performance. You can do a lot to help it improve when it falls below standard. Therefore, when you analyze the potential reasons for a performance problem, you need to also look in the mirror and examine your own influence—often the toughest challenge.

Who is to blame is not the issue. The issue *is* what your influence has been. Managers influence employee performance by their efforts of input and consequences. **Input** is what is done to get performance started. Examples include:

- requests
- directions
- orders
- training
- policies
- procedures
- goal setting
- schedules

Consequences are what is or is not done after performance has happened, that influences the way it will happen again. Examples include:

- feedback
- praise
- criticism
- bonuses
- raises
- recognition
- rewards
- discipline
- threats
- inattention

EXAMINE YOUR INFLUENCE (continued)

When a difficult-employee situation exists, as manager, you need to look at your efforts of input and consequence on that employee's performance. In addition to changes the employee needs to do, a little or a lot, change on your part will be required to help that employee improve. It rarely works for you to maintain the status quo. Remember, you have a problem on your hands; what you have done so far has not been good enough.

Look at your pattern of communication with the employee; change may be needed there. Ask yourself these two questions when you make efforts to communicate with this person: (1) What do I do when we have good conversations? (2) What do I do when we have poor conversations? Very simply, look to do more of your behaviors in question 1 and less of your behaviors in question 2.

In analyzing the problem, also look at patterns that may exist with the employee. For example, ask yourself a few key questions:

- How often is this problem displayed?
- Are other areas of the job affected?
- Have significant changes occurred in or outside of work?
- Have other employees encountered similar difficulties?

Avoid psychoanalysis as you look for potential patterns and reasons. The employee will often help you answer these questions when you meet. Stay out of employees' heads. Do not try to guess what they think, why they act the way they do, or what their motives are. This is minefield territory which can lead, most certainly, to conflict. Stick to examining the performance issues at hand. You want to diffuse the tension, not increase it.

CASE STUDY #2

Practice by analyzing the following case:

Frank

Frank is one of the veterans who works for Roger. He has been a steady and moderate performer in the department for over three years. Over three months ago, Roger gave him some new responsibilities.

During the last few weeks, Roger noticed a drop in Frank's work. Frank's errors have increased and tasks, especially associated with the new responsibilities, have been getting done later and later. Roger talked to Frank briefly a couple of times to see if there were any problems, but both times Frank said everything was fine.

After hearing grumbling from other employees about mistakes Frank continues to make, Roger sat down with him to explore the problem. Frank said he had been worried about his son, who was having difficulty in high school. Much of the discussion then focused on Frank's son, with Roger offering advice on how to take care of the problem. "I can relate," Roger said. "I had a tough time getting through high school myself." The meeting ended with Frank saying he would try harder.

CASE STUDY ANALYSIS

CASE STUDY ANALYSIS

1. Identify the performance problem(s).

2. What are the potential reasons for the problem, including possible patterns with Frank's performance?

3. What management influences have been occurring?

4. What recommended changes would you give to Roger to do?

Check your responses with those of the author, found on pages 72 and 73.

STEP 4: DEFINE THE EXPECTED PERFORMANCE STANDARD

Performance problems do not fix themselves without corrective intervention. This requires you to have a conference with the difficult employee, to work out an improvement plan. Being prepared ahead of time will make a difference in turning your conference into a success. The remaining steps of the Intervention Model will be useful in that conference.

Before working out ways with the employee on how to improve his or her performance, you need to define performance standards. A standard tells specifically what the level of performance or expectations should be. For example, it should say, "The standard is to be at your desk, ready to work, by 8:00" rather than "Be to work on time."

Standards should be stated in clear and measurable terms. Never assume employees already know what is expected. Quite often the problem is that the manager has not communicated what the performance standards are. If the manager is not sure, you can bet the employee will not know what is really expected.

STEP 5: EXPLORE IDEAS FOR A SOLUTION

Once expectations or standards are defined, the level of performance needed is known; figuring out how to get there is more readily apparent. In your preparation before meeting with the problem employee, have a few ideas in mind about what the employee can do to improve and what you, as manager, can do to help. Remember, when you explored possible reasons for the problem, you also came up with possible ideas for a solution. (Refer to pages 67 to 71.)

When you meet with the employee, brainstorm together. First take a *what if* approach—any idea is possible. After your ideas have been exhausted, discuss their merits and evaluate which action plans will work best.

The key here is to allow for and encourage, employee involvement. You may be surprised, but employees often come up with better ideas than you have on how they can improve their performance and where you can best help. Employee commitment is greater when they have an opportunity to be a part of the solution.

Often, managers tell employees what *not* to do and *never* develop a plan with them on what *to* do. Telling difficult employees they have been problems, without working out ways to improve *with* them, cuts down on possibilities for positive improvement. Being corrective, not punitive, means working with them on how to go, not just telling them to stop.

STEP 6: WRITE THE PLAN FOR IMPROVEMENT

Once you have had the discussion on how to improve, the last step of the intervention effort is to put the ideas you have agreed upon into a written plan. The plan should spell out the following points:

I. The goal or area that needs improvement

II. The step-by-step action plans

The plans should identify what the employee is to do and, as appropriate, what the manager is to do. Include target dates, which provide a timetable as to when efforts are to be accomplished.

III. Consequences—positive and, as needed, negative

Possible positive consequences for achieving improvement may include a letter of recognition to the personnel file, a chance to take on greater responsibilities, the opportunity to work on a special assignment, greater autonomy.

If verbal counseling does not yield improvement, define, as appropriate, what the next step of negative consequences would be. This would include formal disciplinary action. Exercise corrective discretion here: This means that sometimes more than one verbal counseling or intervention effort is needed before disciplinary action serves as a fair and logical consequence for poor performance.

IV. Follow-up time

Set a date when you and the employee will sit down and fully review his or her progress. Allow flexibility (e.g., we will meet again within 45 days) so you can intervene sooner if performance continues to decline.

STEP 6: WRITE THE PLAN FOR IMPROVEMENT (continued)

What should you do with the written plan?

The written plan is the road map for improvement for *you and your employee's use.* Except for cases involving formal disciplinary action, it is best kept out of the employee's official personnel file.

For many employees, anything put into their files about their performance is either a formal evaluation or a warning letter. Not surprising then, they are frequently apprehensive when anything is written about performance for the file.

Remember, the idea here is to improve performance, not to increase apprehension. The product being developed by the two of you is a *working plan* for the two of you—an important part or objective in the effort to manage performance. If the plan goes in the *file,* as part of this counseling and coaching effort, it has now become a punitive, rather than corrective, tool.

At the same time, your work with the employee is *on the record;* do not treat it as something that does not really count. The improvement plan itself serves as documentation of the performance concern. Concern prompted the plan; and you are developing the plan to eliminate the concern.

Stress this point with the employee. Without putting the improvement plan in writing, many of the ideas discussed are likely to be forgotten or misunderstood. Very simply, plans put into writing are more likely to happen. You can let the employee help write the plan, then, each of you should retain a copy to use for reviewing and guiding the improvement of performance.

P A R T III

The Intervention Conference

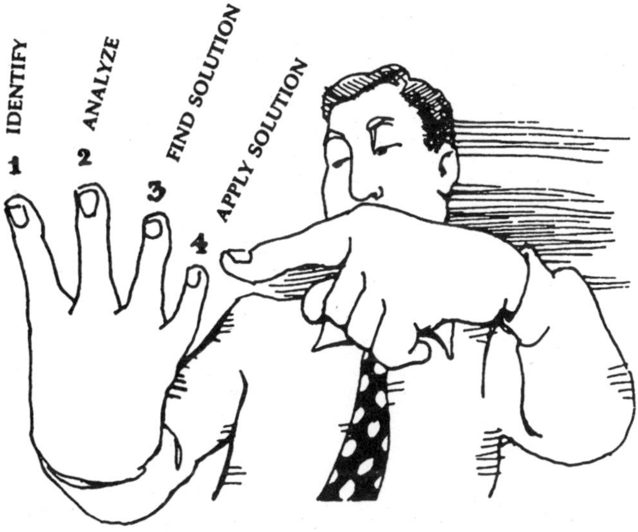

THE CONFERENCE AGENDA

Preparation is the key to having a productive intervention conference with the difficult employee. Having an agenda set for yourself will help you conduct the meeting; it will keep you organized and in control. If you are not, you will find it difficult to develop a corrective action plan with the employee. Here is an outline of a practical agenda to follow. It incorporates the six steps of the Intervention Model:

Conference Agenda

I INTRODUCTION

A. State the purpose of the meeting.
B. State what you want to accomplish.

II REPORT THE PROBLEM

A. Step 1: Identify and define the performance problem.
B. Step 2: Explain the impact of the problem.

III EXPLORE THE CAUSES OF THE PROBLEM

A. Listen to employee thoughts and reactions to what you have reported.
B. Step 3: Analyze the reasons for the problem.
   1. Discuss reasons with employee; test your own ideas, as appropriate.
   2. Discuss your influence on the situation.

IV CORRECTIVE ACTIONS

A. Step 4: Define the expected performance standard(s).
B. Step 5: Explore ideas for a solution.
C. Step 6: Write the plan for improvement.

V CLOSE

A. Recap key points and review your plan to finalize it.
B. Make sure a follow-up meeting is set.

THE CONFERENCE AGENDA (continued)

It is best to keep the introduction for the meeting brief. Your purpose is to address a concern you have with the employee's performance; this helps set a serious tone for the meeting. Your goal is to develop a plan *with* the employee to help improve performance; this helps give the meeting a positive intent.

Follow the agenda and report the performance problem, complete with examples that help define what it is about. You will want to talk first, to start the conference off. However, avoid talking too long, so you do not turn the session into a lecture. Get to the point, for the news needs to be heard by the employee before any meaningful discussion can begin. This also helps to establish your control of the meeting.

Often, after you explain the impact of the problem, the employee acknowledges the problem. It is vital to get the employee's acknowledgment of the problem before you discuss corrective actions. The problem employee does not have to agree with your assessment of the situation, but must at least accept it; otherwise, efforts to improve performance are not likely to be taken seriously.

Avoid dwelling too much on the problem, and do not look for major confessions; a mere "okay" or "yes" by the employee will do.

If the employee is resistant or does not show signs of acknowledgment, move to Step 4 and define the performance standard. Then tell the employee firmly and with concern, "The current level of your performance, as I have reported, is below the standard just defined. That is not acceptable. The goal of this meeting is to work with you to bring your performance up to standard. While you do not have to agree with everything I have told you, if you do not acknowledge that a problem exists, achieving improvement and success in this job will not occur."

As you begin Part III of the conference agenda, avoid rebutting every employee reaction to what you reported. Some employees may vent, which often serves as an emotional release that helps them focus on the performance issue at hand. Engaging in a heated debate may escalate tensions and prevent efforts to reach a workable solution.

As the employee reacts, keep tensions diffused, listen to understand both the feelings and concerns he or she expresses. This information may prove to be very helpful in analyzing the reasons for the problem. If you need to respond to a comment, do so by stating your understanding of the employee's remarks first. Showing understanding of someone else's concerns is often the best way to get that person to understand yours.

If the venting turns into abuse, be firm; remind the employee that you want a discussion, but will not tolerate an argument. Keep yourself in control and stick to your agenda. Remember, be firm, fair and care.

INTERVENTION CONFERENCE CHECKLIST

Here is a checklist for you to follow when you prepare the intervention conference:

Outline Your Agenda

- ☐ 1. Identify the problem in one sentence.
- ☐ 2. Give supporting examples that define the performance problem.
- ☐ 3. Explain, in specific terms, the impact of the problem.
- ☐ 4. List potential reasons for the problem.
- ☐ 5. Explore your own influence on the employee's performance.
- ☐ 6. Define the expected performance standard.
- ☐ 7. Brainstorm and list potential changes and ways to improve performance, including what the employee can do and what you can do.

Other Steps

- ☐ 1. Organize any relevant documentation you need to show the employee (e.g., attendance records, written work, feedback from customers).
- ☐ 2. Set a time for the meeting and ensure privacy.
- ☐ 3. Consult with appropriate parties in advance, as needed (e.g., Human Resources or your manager).
- ☐ 4. Anticipate possible employee reactions and how you could handle them.

Anticipating potential reactions by the difficult employee is like having an umbrella ready on a cloudy day, in case it rains. Knowing the person, think out how you may handle specific reactions so you remain in control and the meeting stays focused. Here are a few possible examples:

- *The employee cries upon hearing about the problem.*

  Possible response—have tissue handy. Slow your pace a little, and keep the discussion moving so the crying is a minor distraction, not a major disruption.

- *The person says very little or is silent.*

  Possible response—ask questions, one at a time, focused on an issue that forces the individual to express thoughts, not one word responses. After asking each question, wait patiently and let the employee fill the silence.

- *The employee complains and says others are at fault.*

  Possible responses—listen carefully; the complaint may have some validity. Then, refocus onto the issues of that person's performance and responsibilities. Keep moving the agenda along.

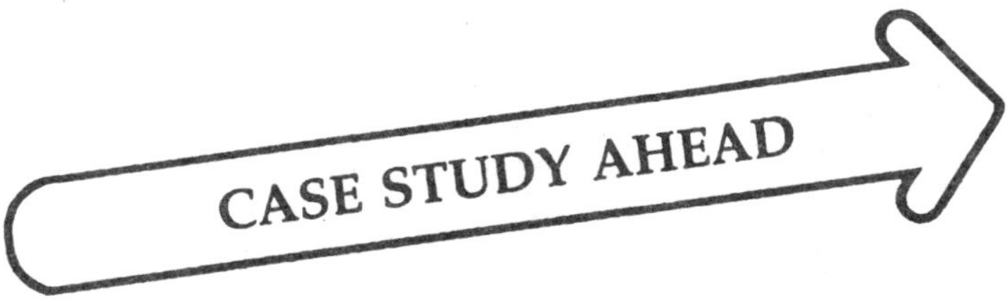

CASE STUDY #3

Practice by analyzing the following case.

Elena

Elena has been in her position as a service representative for a couple of years. She has mastered most of the main tasks associated with her job.

Her behavior has grown increasingly difficult to deal with, especially for her manager. She frequently bounces back and forth in her moods, from apathetic to complaining. For example, on many occasions she spends much of the day sitting quietly at her desk or moving slowly about the office with her chin down. Little work gets done on these days. At other times, she complains how nothing is ever right or how others are to blame for mistakes.

Elena's work is suffering. Her output is one-third less than the amount of work she used to do, and the quality of her work has decreased sharply. Her errors are up, and she sometimes handles conversations with callers discourteously (i.e., she has yelled a couple of times on the phone, her voice tone has been abrupt, and she hung up on a customer last week).

Recently, while working on a project with some co-workers, she made many mistakes that required much of the work to be re-done and a deadline to be pushed back. Needless to say, Elena's manager is concerned about her performance.

CASE STUDY ANALYSIS

Apply the Intervention Model and outline the steps you, as manager, will take to improve this problem employee situation. Include a possible improvement plan. Check your response with the author's on pages 74 and 75.

Step 1 ______________________________

____

____

Step 2 ______________________________

____

____

Step 3 ______________________________

____

____

Step 4 ______________________________

____

____

Step 5 ______________________________

____

____

Step 6 ______________________________

____

____

CASE STUDY ANAYLSIS (continued)

Outline your intervention effort with a performance problem situation you currently have or had in the past.

Step 1 ______________________________

____

____

Step 2 ______________________________

____

____

Step 3 ______________________________

____

____

Step 4 ______________________________

____

____

Step 5 ______________________________

____

____

Step 6 ______________________________

____

____

PART IV

Disciplinary Action and Termination

DISCIPLINARY ACTION AGENDA

Here is a simple agenda to follow in conducting a disciplinary conference with the difficult employee:

I. Introduction of Action

- Present documentation for employee to read

II. Review Highlights

- The problem and past efforts to address it
- The expected standards of performance
- Secure employee understanding

III. Explore Ideas to Gain Improvement

Note: While you have stated what steps the employee needs to take to improve performance in the written warning, remain flexible. In your discussion here, if better ideas come up, adjust or add to the document accordingly.

IV. Review Consequences

- Offer appropriate support and review follow-up time

THE WHATS AND WHENS OF DISCIPLINE

Discipline is sometimes required as part of the efforts to correct employee performance problems. Disciplinary action is defined as a formal action of consequences, documented for the record and carried out, to halt a performance problem from continuing and to point it in a direction of improvement.

Formal Disciplinary Action

Formal disciplinary action is most effective when it comes as a logical consequence: (1) when efforts to counsel and improve performance have not yielded sufficient progress, or (2) when actions by the employee were of a serious nature (i.e., forms of gross misconduct). Depending on the severity of the incident, discharge for such employee actions may be justified. The consequences for not improving need to be spelled out in advance, during the counseling efforts—this is key for minimizing surprises and being corrective. Even in cases of a severe nature, disciplinary action should not come as a surprise, unless these kinds of problems are normally avoided by the organization.

When carrying out formal disciplinary action, follow the steps of the intervention model. In this case, your documentation needs to be prepared in advance of the conference. This time, the plan goes into the employee's personnel file. As part of this preparation, consult with your own manager and your human resources manager. The idea here is not to operate in a vacuum, but to have the support of key people, to make sure your actions are appropriate and in-line with your organization's policies. Human resources staff can be helpful in reviewing your documentation to make sure it sounds clear and it is corrective in its tone. The following page contains a guide for writing disciplinary documentation.

Guide for Disciplinary Action Documentation

Narrative Outline

(Heading—List the step in the Discipline Plan)

Step 1: First Written Warning

TO: Employee
FROM: Manager

I. Opening

- State that this action is a formal disciplinary action.

II. Problem Identification

- State specifically the problem exhibited-the performance issue (the work, attendance, and behavior) involved. Give examples as needed to add clarification. Also, make reference to the fact that previous discussions or counseling sessions about the problem have taken place.

III. State Expectations

- Spell out clearly what the person is expected to do or accomplish to correct the problem. List out each relevant expectation and action plan for improvement. (These plans can be modified in the discussion with the employee.)

  1. ______________________________
  2. ______________________________
  3. ______________________________

- As appropriate, state what you will do to help the person meet the expectations.
- Offer words of encouragement as appropriate.

IV. Close

- Give time frame as to when you will get together to review progress, i.e., ''within 30 days or less.'' Allow yourself the flexibility to meet sooner if need be.
- Add statement indicating consequences if improvement does not occur, i.e., ''if progress is not shown, further disciplinary action will result, up to and including termination.''

ACKNOWLEDGED: ______________________________ DATE: ____________________
(Employee Signature)

NOTE:

1) Unless the action is for Recommendation for Termination, make the tone of the letter corrective, not punitive.

2) Review all letters of documentation with Human Resources prior to conducting the conference.

PROGRESSIVE DISCIPLINE POLICIES

Since the 1980s, as it affects the employment relationship, the most common lawsuit against employers has been wrongful termination. Employees win these cases more often than not, generally due to mistakes the employers have made in handling performance problem situations such as:

- Little or no documentation of the actual problem
- Little or no effort to tell the employee what to do to improve
- Arbitrary actions that are seen as quite unfair (i.e., no logical consequences, promises not kept, punishment to employee for exercising employment rights such as filing a workers' compensation claim)

When employers have progressive discipline plans and use them to guide their managers in handling problem employee situations, legal liabilities are minimized. These plans or policies spell out the steps of consequences for poor performance. They guide managers to work with employees to correct and improve these problems. An example of such a policy starts on the next page.

Sample Policy: Progressive Discipline Plan

INTRODUCTION

All XYZ Company employees are expected to maintain high standards of job performance and to support company efforts to maintain a professional and positive work environment. Should job performance, related to behavior, work and/or attendance, not meet required standards, the company generally seeks to utilize corrective measures to resolve such problems. This Progressive Discipline Plan is designed to provide supervisors guidance in working with their employees to correct performance problems.

VERBAL COUNSELING

Supervisors are expected to hold informal verbal counseling sessions with their employees, as performance problems arise, before initiating formal disciplinary action. The intent of these sessions is to work together to help improve performance, including development of improvement plans.

When counseling efforts have failed to correct a performance problem, formal disciplinary action may be initiated, according to the following steps:

STEP 1: WRITTEN WARNING

STEP 2: FINAL WARNING

STEP 3: RECOMMENDATION FOR TERMINATION

Before carrying out disciplinary action, supervisors are to prepare formal documentation and consult with Human Resources. Documentation for Step 1 and Step 2 Warnings needs to detail these key points: the performance problem, the expectations or standards to be met, efforts needed for the employee to improve performance, and a follow-up time frame, within 30 to 90 days, to review progress. Consequences, if the problem is not corrected, are also included in the documentation.

After communicating a disciplinary action to the employee, the documentation is forwarded to the employee's personnel file. Employees who are on formal warning are not eligible to receive pay increases, promotional opportunities or other special incentives or awards.

If the actions of Step 2 do not result in the necessary improvement, a supervisor may recommend termination of the problem employee. The supervisor first documents the reasons that justify termination. Approval for such action must come from Human Resources and the department head. If an investigation is needed before a final decision can be made, the employee may be suspended during this period, with or without pay.

SAMPLE POLICY (continued)

SEVERE CLAUSE

Actions of a severe nature are not to be tolerated and will result in formal disciplinary action, up to and including termination. Examples of such severe incidents are:

- Gross misconduct or insubordination
- Abuse or damage of company property
- Being intoxicated or under the influence of a controlled substance
- Revealing trade or other confidential business information to unauthorized parties
- Unauthorized expenditure of company funds
- Fighting, threatening or harassing another employee, vendor or customer

For these examples or any other incidents of a severe nature, supervisors are to document the actions that occurred and recommend to Human Resources and the department head the disciplinary action desired. If there is a need to have the employee removed from the workplace while such an incident is being investigated, supervisors may suspend the employee. Once a final decision is reached, the employee is to be notified of the outcome.

THE ISSUE OF TERMINATION

Terminating an employee due to a performance problem is one of the most difficult tasks for any manager. Termination works best when it comes as the last step of good faith efforts to try to improve employee performance or is the consequence for employee actions of a severe nature. Keep this context in mind and avoid these *nevers* when handling termination situations:

1. Never make the decision on your own. Consult with your manager and Human Resources before acting. Again, you want termination to be the most correct and fair decision. Therefore, do not act in a vacuum.

2. Never carry out a termination unless all documentation is in order. Do not procrastinate, but hasty actions to get rid of someone may come back to haunt you.

3. Never terminate an employee while you are in a state of anger or distress. When the time comes to deliver the difficult news, you want to be emotionally in control.

Avoiding these nevers of termination is important in minimizing potential legal liabilities and charges of discrimination. Here are a few additional tips to follow to constructively handle the termination conference with the employee:

- Relate the termination as the final step of consequences. In doing so, review past efforts taken.
- Give the specific reasons this action is being taken. Present them in documented form.
- Let the employee have the chance to talk; be willing to listen. In most cases, this situation is not easy for the employee. Allowing some communication to occur relieves emotions and keeps the meeting on a human level.
- Focus any discussion about the reasons for the termination on the person's unacceptable performance, not on the person.
- If you anticipate a potentially tense meeting, have a third person present (i.e., someone from Human Resources or your manager), to help diffuse possible tensions.
- Stay in control. Conduct the meeting at a time of day that will be least disruptive to the work environment.

Remember, It Is All About Improving Performance

In dealing with the difficult employee, never lose sight of your goal to correct the performance problem. This effort of intervention is not easy, but it is a critical part of your job, in effectively managing performance. Doing anything less costs an organization too much in productivity, morale and potential lawsuits.

Managers who realize this and work hard to improve performance problems most often get the best results—improved performance. Working to be firm, to be fair and to care works, and employees often recognize these efforts. When employees become problems, let them know very simply that you do not spend time taking "specks off rotten apples."

PART V

Author's Responses

EXERCISE #1: ANSWERS

1. On two important assignments the past month, Mary's lack of cooperation has hurt her performance. On both occasions, employees came to her for assistance; instead they received comments in a sharp tone that said, "I'm too busy right now to bother with what you want." In meetings with the others on the team to plan out the assignments, Mary pushed her ideas as the way to do the job. When others expressed different ideas, she responded by telling them that their ideas would not work and she would not discuss the points further.

2. On four occasions during the past three weeks, customers have remarked negatively about Steve's manner. A couple said he would not look at them, and they had to repeat their requests twice to get his attention. Another person stated that Steve was abrupt, telling her, "Hurry up and make up your mind. I haven't got all day." Still another customer said that because of noise in the back area, Steve kept yelling at other employees to "shut up!" while the customer was attempting to explain what he needed.

CASE STUDY #1: ANSWERS

JIM'S CASE

Labels About Jim:

- Disagreeable
- Disorganized
- Lacks drive and motivation
- Not very reliable

Brief Identification of Jim's Performance Problems:

- Difficulty in taking directions or accepting new ideas
- Twice as long as average in making customer deliveries
- Plans out deliveries poorly—does not take map into new area, makes inefficient use of time in carrying out deliveries
- Has to be told to get to work
- Takes long lunch hours, 15 minutes over the allotted time

EXERCISE #2: ANSWERS

Praise, Criticism, or Constructive Feedback

1. Criticism
2. Constructive feedback
3. Praise
4. Constructive feedback
5. Criticism

Feedback Scenarios:

1. **George**

   George, you are off to a great start on your job. I have noticed that you have learned five of the key tasks (name them) of the job. You have gotten everything done on time and correctly. Best of all, you have shown initiative to pitch in and help the other staff when they have needed it. Keep up the good work!

2. **Melissa**

   Melissa, I have some concerns regarding your performance with a couple of important customer service duties. First, the number of calls you handled the past month is 20% below standard. In addition, I noticed the customer file records are more than two weeks behind schedule.

   Note: In the Melissa scenario, avoid giving a "Yes, but" type message. Her greeting customers warmly is not the issue in this case.

3. **Roberto**

   Roberto, I have a concern regarding your attendance. The records show you have had ten days of absences, each a separate incident, during the past three months. This is a high frequency of absence for our department; it causes the other staff to do extra work to cover your desk.

EXERCISE #3: ANSWERS

Performance Assessments

1. They do not know how or what they should do. Why?

- The employee lacks training or instruction on how to do the task(s).
- Expectations, or clear direction as to what to do, have not been communicated.
- People assume the employee knows how or what to do, leaving the employee reluctant to ask questions.
- A narrow view exists of what one's own job entails. "That's not my job," is sometimes voiced by such an employee.

What can the manager do to help?

- Provide training for the employee to learn how, and allow for practice so she or he can master the task proficiently.
- Give direction and explanations as to how things are to be done and what is expected.
- Encourage questions: Tell employees to come to you when they have questions and be available to answer them when they come.
- Plan projects and assignments together. Give a picture as to the role the person needs to perform.

2. The reward or consequence is for not doing what should be done. Why?

- Efforts made in the past received little or no response. Therefore, the employee's reaction is "why bother to try?"
- When errors have been made, the manager or another employee has corrected them.
- Whenever the employee resists taking on tough tasks, he or she is given easier ones to do instead.
- If difficult behavior in getting along with others has been displayed, the employee has received more autonomy and praise for how well the tasks get done.

What can the manager do to help?

- Give positive feedback and express appreciation for good efforts made, especially on difficult assignments.
- Let employees correct their own errors and help them learn how to correct them.
- Provide employees training and assistance to do tough tasks. Hold them accountable for doing them. Once mastered, a task becomes less difficult.
- Let employees know the impact of their difficult behavior. Set limits on their freedoms and responsibilities, to focus them on bringing the behavior under control.

3. They think they are doing just fine. Why?

- Feedback is seldom given. For most employees, no news means good news.
- If news is given on performance, it tends to be given well after the fact and usually in general or vague terms; therefore, it does not have much impact or value to the individual.

What can the manager do to help?

- Track employee performance on a regular basis, and provide constructive feedback in a timely manner.
- Set objectives. Periodically (e.g., quarterly), review progress. Include self-evaluation as part of that meeting. Self-evaluation, combined with manager feedback, can keep both parties aware of how performance is progressing.

4. They think their way, not your way, is better, and it is not. Why?

- The need for change or going your way is not seen or readily understood.
- The employee has been doing his or her job the same way for a long time and thinks that way is just fine.

What can the manager do to help?

- Explain the reasons and benefits for doing things differently.
- Involve the employee in planning to make the change happen. Those involved in planning the changes that will affect their work are more likely to support the changes.
- Where possible, show the person how the new way can work.

5. There is no negative consequence for poor performance. Why?

- The employee receives average or better performance evaluations and pay raises to match.
- The employee still gets to do favorable assignments.
- The employee receives as much, if not more, attention than others in the group, but as far as actions carried out, status quo remains.

What can the manager do to help?

- Give honest feedback and performance evaluations and appropriate raises—little or none at all.
- Set consequences or limits, and let the employee know them in advance. Then, if improvement does not happen, follow through. In particular, deny special assignments or privileges the employee normally gets to do.

EXERCISE #3: ANSWERS (continued)

6. They have obstacles limiting their performance. Why?

- They lack the resources or know-how to do the job.
- They have been given responsibility, such as to lead a project, without the authority to go with it.
- They have been given conflicting sets of directions (e.g., first from you and then from your boss).
- Other employees, especially in other departments, are not doing their part or are causing interference in work getting done.

What can the manager do to help?

- Listen to the causes of the obstacles and look for ways to remove them. Sometimes, this involves dealing with peer managers to get the cooperation needed. Other times, this help may be in the form of resources, training or guidance the employee needs to do the job.
- Announce to those involved that your employee is in charge of the project and their support is expected.
- Talk to your boss to clear up conflicting directions, and to establish a clear channel of communication. Projects work best when you are the focal point for informing employees of what to do. Do not hesitate to remind your boss of this fact.

7. They do not want to, or know why they should, do the job. Why?

- Previous efforts to accomplish a particular assignment, especially a difficult one, went unrecognized.
- Since they see no reason or importance for doing the particular task, they do not think the effort is worth taking.
- They have grown dissatisfied with part or much of their job.

What can the manager do to help?

- Give positive feedback and recognition for efforts made.
- Discuss with employees the importance and benefits of doing a particular job. Address any concerns they may have.
- Where possible, work with the employee to add new challenges that may be more stimulating, to the job.
- Plan and problem solve together. This allows for employee involvement and makes the importance of a particular assignment much easier to understand.
- If the above efforts do not yield results, set limits and do not allow substandard performance to occur. Not doing what has to be done is still not acceptable.

8. They fear a negative consequence. Why?

- They fear if they do something wrong, you may lose your temper. Often this feeling is because of the way they have seen you react to problems or mistakes in the past. A loud or very emotional reaction to negative situations instills a sense of fear.
- They fear they will be looked upon as stupid if they ask questions, so they do not.
- They fear failure, so they avoid situations that are new or require them to take risks.

What can the manager do to help?

- Avoid sarcasm, yelling and emotional outbursts when mistakes or problems occur. Stay in control.
- If mistakes are made, help employees learn how to correct them. Stay away from an atmosphere of punishing mistakes.
- Encourage questions on an ongoing basis. When you see they are reluctant to try something, discuss their concerns and encourage their efforts to go forward.

9. They are, in essence, punished for doing what they are supposed to do. Why?

- *Shoot the messenger* syndrome occurs sometimes. They report the news they are supposed to report. However, when it contains bad news, your emotional outburst is usually the result, which they perceive as punishment.
- When they take initiative that does not work out, or raise ideas you do not like or agree with, they are chastised or put down for their efforts.
- They get labelled as the *old reliable* employees. As a result, they get the most work and the most difficult or unpleasant assignments in the group.

EXERCISE #3: ANSWERS (continued)

What can the manager do to help?

- Keep your emotions under control when employees report what is happening. As manager, you need information flowing to you; therefore, recognize that the news will not always be good. Let the messenger live.
- When employees' initiatives do not work out, appreciate the initiatives. Then, help employees learn from their mistakes and give guidance as to where and how initiative should be taken. If you punish employees when these situations happen, they will wait to be told what to do; they will not think for themselves.
- When an employee's ideas are not good ones, discuss them and explain why they are not appropriate. Express appreciation for their effort, but feel free to agree to disagree. When employees are put down for suggesting ideas, their creativity dies instantly.
- Distribute workload and assignments more evenly among your staff. Reward reliable employees by allowing them to do some of the favorable tasks.

10. They think something else is more important. Why?

- You have not made the priorities of the job clear.
- Nearly every assignment they are given is labelled as urgent. What is truly important is cloudy.
- Priorities have changed, but they have not been informed. Consequently, they are spending too much time on less important issues.
- Other interests or concerns unrelated to the job occupy their time or attention.

What can the manager do to help?

- Discuss with employees what the priorities are and what is most important to tackle first—you may need to sort that out for yourself first.
- Plan with employees how key assignments or projects are to be carried out. Communicate in advance when changes are to occur.
- Focus employees' attention on what is important to getting the job done. Allow for a conditional accountability as appropriate; if you accommodate someone (adjusting schedules, granting a little time off) so he or she can take care of an outside distraction, do so with the condition that the person's attention must return to the job.

CASE STUDY #2: ANSWERS

Frank's Case

1. The performance problem

Frank's accuracy and timeliness with his work are both below standard. Errors have been on the increase, and assignments are getting done later and later.

2. Potential reasons and patterns

The turning point with Frank's performance may be linked to when he took on the new responsibilities. Potentially, the main reasons for his poor performance are:

a. *He does not know how.*
When the new responsibilities were assigned, no training was given with them. Frank's behavior, in response to Roger's inquiries if any problem exists, may indicate a reluctance to ask questions or ask for help.

b. *Something else is more important.*
The problems with his son in school are certainly bothering Frank and may be taking his attention away from doing a quality job.

c. *He thinks he is doing just fine.*
Throughout the last few months, Frank has received little direct feedback from his manager, Roger, about his performance problem. Even in their meeting together, Roger said little as to exactly what the performance problem was.

3. Management influences

Roger may be lacking in some of his efforts to provide input and consequences for Frank. He does not appear to have provided any training or guidance when the new responsibilities were assigned to Frank. He has given little feedback or direct attention about his performance.

In their conference together, Roger played more the role of counselor or therapist than that of manager. He focused much of the discussion on how to work out problems with Frank's son, not on Frank's performance.

CASE STUDY #2: ANSWERS (continued)

4. Recommendations for Roger with Frank

First, stay away from being Frank's family therapist. If Roger knows of resources in the community that can help, and Frank is looking for that, refer him to them.

Give Frank constructive feedback on what his performance problem is, as well as on its impact. Then, in working out a plan of improvement with Frank, explore his knowledge and skill with the new responsibilities. See if any training or assistance is needed. Do not accept Frank's response that everything is fine.

If Frank needs time to take care of problems with his son, accommodate him, as appropriate. Then, refocus his attention on the importance of doing his job accurately and timely.

CASE STUDY #3: ANSWERS

Elena's Case

1. Performance problem:

- Output down, errors up and discourteous service to customers.
- Mood swings are signs that a performance problem is developing; they are not the problem itself. To express concern about the way Elena has been acting may be fine to bring to her attention, but to dwell on or emphasize it will focus you on personality and away from performance issues.

Examples to define the problem:

- Output one-third off standard. Show her the supporting data.
- Show and explain examples of the errors she has made, including those she did on the group project.
- Share observations and direct feedback from customers about her manner on calls. Demonstrate, as needed, especially the tone she used on some of her calls.

2. Impact of performance problem:

- Explain the effect of poor service on the group and on the business.
- Explain how her low output and quality of her work are affecting her productivity, as well as the group members' confidence in working with Elena. If others are having to pick up the slack, provide examples.

3. Possible reasons to explore:

a. She does not want to or know why she should do the job (Reason #7)
Since Elena has been doing the same tasks for two years, there is a strong possibility that she has grown bored or dissatisfied with much of her job. Potentially, much of her previous efforts have gone unnoticed. The manager's influence, in terms of feedback and recognition, need to be examined.

b. The reward or consequence is for not doing the job. (Reason #2)
Related to the reason above, the kinds of responses given to Elena's past efforts need to be explored. In addition, the manager needs to analyze how he or she has been handling errors Elena has been making. If they have been ignored or others have been correcting them, Elena may feel no need to try.

4. Performance standards to define:

- Level of output required
- Acceptable error rate and quality of work desired
- Courteous and friendly service to customers on the phone

POSSIBLE IMPROVEMENT PLAN FOR ELENA

State goals desired:

Relate goals to output, work quality and level of customer service desired.

Action plans:

1. The manager will spend four hours with Elena over the next week to closely review how she works—in particular, to identify the source of her errors.

2. On errors Elena makes, where assistance is needed to learn how to correct them, the manager will help. All others are to be corrected by Elena herself. Elena is to keep a record of her errors, for at least the first month, so she remains aware and does not repeat them. The manager will review errors with Elena weekly, for the first month, to track improvement in quality.

3. The manager will role play calls with Elena, to review how to handle them in a courteous and friendly manner. If Elena desires, a small mirror will be provided to remind her to keep a smile in her voice. Periodically, the manager will listen in on some calls with her.

4. Elena will work with her manager to develop a criteria sheet for Elena to assess herself periodically on how she handles service calls. The manager will also use this evaluation form when observing calls and will have the rest of the staff make use of it as well—much the same way a good sales manager evaluates a staff making sales calls.

5. Elena will work up to the desired output standard, in increment levels each week, to reach her goal by the end of the month. The manager will review output standards to ensure that requirements are reasonable.

6. If, for two months, Elena shows improvement and maintains the performance levels needed, she will be given varied responsibilities to add more challenge to her job; her other tasks will be balanced accordingly; some of the tasks she will get to do include:

   - Help manager with special projects.
   - Train new staff people on the job.
   - Investigate complex customer inquiries.

Follow-up:

Elena and her manager will formally review her progress, once a month for the next two months. If action plans are met, reviews of overall performance will be quarterly thereafter.

Note: This improvement plan assumes these ideas were worked out with Elena.

NOTES

NOTES

TITLES IN THE VIVA-CRISP 50 MINUTE SERIES

ISBN	Title / Author	Price Rs. 99/- Each
ADULT LEARNING		
— 8176495131	**Basic Business Math** by Richard P. Truchon	
— 8176495697	**Formatting Letters and Reports** by Eleanor Davidson	
— 8176496901	**Improve Your Reading Improve Your Job** by Jeanne Miller	
— 817649710X	**Study Skills Strategies** by Uelaine Lengefeld	
— 8176497118	**Successful Life Long Learning** by Robert Steinbach	
— 8176497320	**Vocabulary Improvement** by Diana Bonet	
CALL CENTER SUCCESS		
— 8176495271	**Call Center Success** by Lloyd C. Finch	
CHANGE		
— 8176495387	**Coping With Workplace Change** by J. Jeffreys	
— 8176495875	**Managing Change at Work** by C. Scott & D. Jaffe	
— 8176495913	**Managing Personal Change** by C. Scott & Dennis Jaffe	
— 8176497282	**Understanding Organizational Change** by L. Fossum	
COACHING AND MENTORING		
— 8176495166	**Be Your Own Coach** by B. Braham & C. Wahl	
— 817649531X	**Coaching and Counseling** by Marianne Minor	
— 8176495328	**Coaching for Development** by Marianne Minor	
— 8176495859	**Making the Most of Being Mentored** by Gordon F. Shea	
— 8176495999	**Mentoring** by Gordon F. Shea	
COMPLIANCE		
— 8176495522	**Disaster Preparedness** by J. Freestone & R. Raab	
CONFLICT RESOLUTION		
— 8176495883	**Managing Disagreement Constructively** by Herbert S. Kindler	
CREATIVITY		
— 8176495417	**Creative Decision Making** by H. B. Gelatt	
— 8176495425	**Creativity in Business** by Carol Kinsey Goman	
CUSTOMER SERVICE		
— 8176496839	**A Positive Guide to Superior Service** by William Martin	
— 8176495018	**Beyond Customer Service** by Richard F. Gerson	
— 8176496863	**Calming Upset Customers** by Rebecca Morgan	
— 8176495441	**Customer Satisfaction** by Dru Scott	
— 8176495921	**Managing Quality Customer Service** by William B. Martin	

	ISBN	Title / Author	Price Rs. 99/- Each
—	8176495972	**Measuring Customer Satisfaction** by R. Gerson	
—	817649691X	**Most Customer Services Start With the Telephone** by Nancy Friedman	

ELECTRONIC COMMUNICATION

—	817649738X	**Writing Effective E-Mail** by Nancy Flynn

FINANCE

—	8176495050	**The Accounting Cycle** by J. Jacquet & W. Miller
—	8176495855	**Basics of Budgeting** by Terry Dickey
—	8176495689	**Financial Analysis** by J. Gill & M. Chatton
—	8176496987	**Personal Financial Fitness** by Allen Klosowski
—	817649707X	**Starting Your New Business** by Charles Martin
—	8176497290	**Understanding Financial Statements** by James Gill

HIRING AND MANAGING

—	817649500X	**50 One-Minute Tips for Recruiting Employees** by Hayes & Ninemeier
—	8176494526	**50 One-Minute Tips for Retaining Employees** by Hayes & NInemeier
—	8176495034	**About Pay** by James F. Carey
—	8176495115	**Attacking Absenteeism** by Lynn Tylczak
—	8176495174	**Behavior-Based Interviewing** by Terry Fitzwater
—	817649559X	**Effective Recruiting Strategies** by R. Visconti & M. Brounstein
—	817649562X	**Employee Suggestion Systems** by C. Martin & R. Bassford
—	8176495751	**High Performance Hiring** by Robert Wendover
—	8176496995	**Personnel Testing** by John Jones
—	8176497037	**Quality Interviewing** by Robert Maddux
—	8176497045	**Recruiting for High Performance** by Robert Wendover
—	8176497363	**Writing a Human Resources Manual** by S. Brock & S. Cabbell

INCREASE EMPLOYEE PERFORMANCE

—	8176495530	**Downsizing Without Disaster** by Lynn Tylczak
—	8176495573	**Effective Performance Appraisals** by Robert B. Maddux
—	8176495638	**Empowerment** by C. Scott & D. Jaffe
—	8176495743	**Handling the Difficult Employee** by Marty Brounstein
—	8176495867	**Managing Anger** by Rebecca Luhn Wolfe
—	8176495891	**Managing for Commitment** by Carol Kinsey Goman
—	8176495905	**Managing Negative People** by S. Michael Kravitz
—	8176496960	**Partners in Performance** by Tony Moglia

ISBN	Title / Author	Price Rs. 99/- Each
	JOBS AND CAREERS	
— 817649528X	**Career Discovery Program** by Elwood N. Chapman	
— 8176495409	**Creating Your Skills Portfolio** by Carrie Straub	
— 8176495565	**Effective Networking** by Venda Raye-Johnson	
— 8176495719	**Getting Hired** by Richard Pinsker	
— 8176494569	**Networking for Success** by Nancy Flynn	
— 8176496944	**Preparing for the Behavior-Based Interview** by T. Fitzwater	
— 8176497002	**Preparing for Your Interview** by Diane Berk	
— 8176497088	**Strategic Resumes** by Marci Mahoney	
— 817649741X	**Your First Thirty Days** by E. Chapman & R. Maddux	
	MANAGEMENT SKILLS	
— 8176495468	**Delegating For Results** by Robert B. Maddux	
— 8176495735	**Goals and Goal Setting** by Larrie A. Rouillard	
— 8176495778	**Improving Your Company Image** by Sylvia Blishak	
— 8176495948	**Managing the Technical Professional** by Herbert Kindler	
— 8176494550	**Multipoint Feedback** by D. Jude-York & S. Wise	
— 8176494577	**Project Management** by Marion E. Haynes	
— 8176497053	**Retaining Your Employees** by B. Wingfield & J. Berry	
— 8176497126	**Successful Negotiation** by Robert B. Maddux	
— 8176497215	**The Ecstatic Buzz of Doing Business** by J. Bado & C. Ivanacic	
— 8176495808	**The Internal Consultant** by Marcia Meislin	
	MANUFACTURING AND INVENTORY	
— 817649514X	**Basics of Inventory Management** by J. Viale	
— 8176495158	**Basics of Manufacturing** by J. Viale	
— 8176495182	**Benchmarking Basics** by James Patterson	
— 8176495212	**Building a Total Quality Culture** by Joe Batten	
— 8176495816	**JIT Forecasting and Master Scheduling** by J. Viale	
— 8176495379	**The Continuously Improving Self** by J. Lickson	
— 8176497258	**TQM** by JoAnn Haberer & M. Webb	
	PEER RELATIONS & APPEARANCE	
— 8176495247	**Business Etiquette & Professionalism** by M. Kay duPont	
— 817649576X	**Improving Peer Relationships** by Norman Hill	
— 8176495786	**Influence** by Elaina Zuker	
— 8176495794	**Influencing Others** by William Nothstine	
— 8176495956	**Managing Upward** by Patti Hathaway	

	ISBN	Title / Author	Price Rs. 99/- Each
—	8176496936	**Office Politics** by Rebecca Luhn Wolfe	
—	8176496979	**Personal Counseling** by R. Knowdell & E. Chapman	
—	8176494593	**Winning at Human Relations** by Elwood N. Chapman	
		PRESENTATION SKILLS	
—	8176495581	**Effective Presentation Skills** by Steve Mandel	
—	8176497185	**Technical Presentation Skills** by Steve Mandel	
—	8176497304	**Using Visual Aids** by C. Raines & L. Williamson	
		PRODUCTIVITY	
—	8176495085	**Achieving Results** by Lorna Riley	
—	8176495093	**Administrative Assistant** by Brenda Bailey-Hughes	
—	8176496820	**Plan Your Work: Work Your Plan** by James Sherman	
—	8176497134	**Successful Self-Management** by Paul R. Timm	
		SALES AND MARKETING	
—	8176496847	**Achieve Large-Budget Marketing Without a Large Budget** by Richard Gerson	
—	8176495204	**Building and Closing the Sale** by V. Thornton	
—	8176495263	**Business Research** by P. Timm & R. Farr	
—	8176495360	**Consultative Sales Power** by Karen Mantyla	
—	817649545X	**Dealing Effectively With the Media** by John Wade	
—	8176495514	**Direct Marketing Techniques** by Lois Geller	
—	8176495603	**Effective Sales Management** by Tom Johnson	
—	8176495964	**Marketing Your Consulting or Professional Services** by D. Karlson	
—	8176497029	**Prospecting: The Key to Sales Success** by Virden Thornton	
—	8176496774	**Sales Training Basics** by Elwood Chapman	
—	8176497339	**Winning the Inner Game of Selling** by Richard Gerson	
		SELF IMPROVEMENT	
—	8176495077	**Achieving Job Satisfaction** by Editors of Crisp Publications, Inc	
—	8176495123	**Attitude** by E. Chapman & W. Mcknight	
—	8176495298	**Clear and Creative Thinking** by Herb Kindler	
—	8176495344	**Concentration** by Sam Horn	
—	8176495433	**Critical Thinking** by Daniel A. Feldman	
—	8176495492	**Developing Positive Assertiveness** by Sam R. Lloyd	
—	8176495506	**Developing Self-Esteem** by Connie Palladino	
—	8176495646	**Ethics in Business** by R. Maddux & D. Maddux	
—	817649688X	**Finding Your Purpose** by Barbara J. Braham	

ISBN	Title / Author	Price Rs. 99/- Each
— 8176495980	**Memory Skills in Business** by Madelyn Burley-Allen	
— 8176497061	**Risk Taking** by Herbert Kindler	
	STRATEGIC DEVELOPMENT	
— 8176496871	**Competency and the Learning Organization** by Donald Shandler	
— 8176495395	**Creating a Learning Organization** by Barbara Braham	
— 8176496758	**Organization Development** by Lenny Ralphs	
— 8176496952	**Organizational Vision, Values and Mission** by Scott, Jaffe & Tobe	
— 8176497142	**Successful Strategic Planning** by Stephen Haines	
— 8176497169	**Systematic Succession Planning** by Rebecca Wolfe	
— 8176494585	**Understanding Leadership Competencies** by Guggenheimer & Szulc	
	STRESS, WELL-BEING & RETIREMENT	
— 817649593X	**Managing Stress for Mental Fitness** by M. Raber & G. Dyck	
— 8176497096	**Stress that Stress That Motivates** by Dru Scott	
	SUPERVISORY SKILLS	
— 8176495042	**Accountability** by Sam R. Lloyd	
— 8176495239	**Building Trust** by Mary Shurtleff	
— 8176495654	**Excellence in Supervision** by Rick Conlow	
— 8176495700	**From Technical Specialist to Supervisor** by Donald Shandler	
— 8176497150	**Supervising for Success** by Tony Moglia	
— 8176497223	**The New Supervisor** by Elwood N. Chapman	
	TEAM BUILDING AND LEADERSHIP	
— 8176495069	**Achieving Consensus** by Jon Scott & Eileen Flanigan	
— 8176495662	**Facilitation Skills for Team Leaders** by C. Martin & D. Hackett	
— 8176495824	**Leadership Skills for Women** by M. Manning & P. Haddock	
— 8176495832	**Learning to Lead** by E. N. Chapman & P. Heim	
— 8176494542	**Motivating at Work** by Twyla Dell	
— 8176496782	**Team Building** by Robert B. Maddux	
— 8176497177	**Team Problem Solving** by Sandy Pokras	
— 8176497312	**Virtual Teaming** by D. Jude-York & L. Davis	
— 8176497347	**Working in Teams** by Sandy Pokras	
	TELEPHONE SKILLS	
— 8176497207	**Telephone Courtesy & Customer Service** by Lloyd C. Finch	
	TIME MANAGEMENT	
— 817649674X	**Office Management** by M. Manning & P. Haddock	
— 8176496766	**Personal Time Management** by Marion E. Haynes	

ISBN	Title / Author	Price Rs. 99/- Each
— 8176497010	**Professionalism in the Office** by Marilyn Manning	
— 8176497231	**The Telephone and Time Management** by Dru Scott	
	TRAINING	
— 8176495026	**50 One-Minute Tips for Trainers** by Carrie Van Daele	
— 8176495352	**Conducting a Needs Analysis** by Geri McArdle	
— 8176495476	**Delivering Effective Training Sessions** by Geri McArdle	
— 8176495484	**Developing Instructional Design** by Geri McArdle	
— 8176495549	**Dynamics of Diversity** by Odette Pollar	
— 8176496898	**Graphics for Presenters** by Lynn Kearny	
— 8176497266	**Training Managers to Train** by David Hayes	
— 8176497274	**Training Methods That Work** by Lois Hart	
— 8176497355	**Working Together** by George Simons	
	VERBAL COMMUNICATION	
— 8176496731	**50 One-Minute Tips to Better Communication** by P. E. Bozek	
— 8176495336	**Communicating With Employees** by Frank M. Corrado	
— 8176495557	**Effective Meeting Skills** by Marion E. Haynes	
— 8176495611	**Emotional Intelligence Works** by M. Kravitz & S. D. Schubert	
— 8176495727	**Giving and Receiving Feedback** by Patti Hathaway	
— 8176495840	**Making Humor Work** by Terry Paulson	
— 8176495107	**The Art of Communicating** by Bert Decker	
— 8176495255	**The Business of Listening** by Diana Bonet	
— 817649724X	**Thinking on Your Feet** by Marlene Caroselli	
	WRITTEN COMMUNICATION	
— 8176495190	**Better Business Writing** by Susan L. Brock	
— 8176495301	**Clear Writing** by Diana Bonet	
— 8176495670	**Fat-Free Writing** by Carol Andrus	
— 8176496928	**Powerful Proofreading Skills** by D. Smith & H. Sutton	
— 8176497193	**Technical Writing in the Corporate World** by H. Estrin & N. Elliot	
— 8176495220	**The Building Blocks of Business Writing** by Jack Swenson	
— 8176497371	**Writing Business Proposals and Reports** by Susan L. Brock	
— 8176497398	**Writing Fitness** by Jack Swenson	
— 8176497401	**Writing That Sells** by Kathleen A. Begley	

Prices are subject to change without notice.